<Run_A_Way>

Manolo Pierson

Reading Sideways Press

Run_A_Way
Manolo Pierson

First published by Reading Sideways Press,
December 2025

Leiden, The Netherlands,
readingsidewayspress.com
readingsidewayspress@gmail.com

This book is copyright. The copyright of the original text belongs to Manolo Pierson. Except for private study, research, criticism or reviews, as permitted under the Copyright Act, no part of this book may be reproduced, stored in a retrieval system or transmitted in any form or by any means without prior written permission. Enquiries should be made to the publisher.

Typeset in Avara and Caudex

Designed by Manolo Pierson
Proofreading by Andy Fuller

READING
SIDEWAYS
PRESS
RSP

Contents

***********Acknowledgments***********

*

****Foreword by Lindsey A.Freeman ****

*
******************* <start> ***************

*
**1.RUNWAY - Spectacle of Exhaustion **

*

*** 2.RUN AWAY - Hyperbolic Striving ***

*
3.RUN A WAY - Dwelling in the Threshold

*
******************<finish> ***************

*
****************Footnotes***************

*
************ Other materials************

Acknowledgments

This text was first written under the supervision of Patricia Reed and Maxime Benvenuto as a master thesis among the Critical Inquiry Lab, a course of Design Academy Eindhoven. I would therefore like to thank everyone that contributed in the discussion regarding the development of this text, starting from my peers, as well as Alvin Arthur, Aster Verrier, Dayna Casey, Desiree Foerster, Gabriel Fontana, Gabriel A.Mahar, Gijs de Boer, James Taylor-Foster, Lua Vollard, Mark Henning, Marthe Prins, Nadim Choufi, Saskia van Stein, Sonia de Jager, Zach Blas and Zuzanna Zgierska.

Acknowledgements to Andy Fuller and Nuraini Juliastuti for their work with Reading Sideways Press, as well as Lindsey A.Freeman for their generousity.

I would also like to thank every person that I could run with so far, with a special mention for trainer Honore Hoedt.

Finally, an obvious salute to family friends and partner for timeless presence and support.

Foreword by Lindsey A. Freeman

Today it is easy to think that our bodies could hide in plain sight as images of themselves or dissolve into data without nuance. Luckily, this book that you are holding in your hand will counter these horrible thoughts. What began as a thesis in search of a method to use high-intensity running to develop a new mode of discernment resulted in a text that gracefully escapes all the concessions to the genre of triumphant running books. Manolo Pierson shows us running doesn't need to be about numb productivity, it can be a counter-rhythm, if you let it.

In his pursuit of resonance, through and with running, Pierson demonstrates how we can replace the stark experience of accelerationism (following the sociologist Hartmut Rosa) with a more expansive feeling of being in time.[1] This doesn't mean we don't still want to go fast. It means constant tracking and data dumps don't keep us going. Even a time, our best time, isn't enough for us for long. We are in hot pursuit to not simply be measured.

We need to feel like we are in and of things. We want new ways of being in our bodies and in the world, and/or we want to return to some of the old ways of embodiment and ways of taking things in. Mostly we want to feel the dynamism of the world and get a sense of what we might do within it, given the particular bodies we are in and the energy we have in any moment in any place in any weather. To do so we train, balance desire and restraint, pour our bodies into kits that flash color, dash across a space. We try to do everything with heart and style.

Pierson's <Run_A_Way> feels good to read because it offers further proof that style is also substance. Good style makes something difficult look less effortful, gives meaningful resonance to actions, and provides a mode to shift the atmosphere of a running race, a room, a page. If you commit to a style or stylistic choice, it takes courage. While style can simply look like freedom, it has consequences both known and unknown. One of the stylistic choices in this book is the creative use of punctuation. As Gertrude Stein wrote, "There are some punctuations that are interesting and some punctuations that are not."[2] While most punctuation marks in this book are just doing their jobs in predictable ways, there are a couple that are up to something. From the start, the angle brackets in the title, <Run_A_Way,> give the impression of runner's legs, knees up, but with one knee pointed forward and the other pointed backwards. This Janus-kneed punctuation is the first indication that this will not be a typical book about sport, following the predictable forward progress trajectory of training, adversity and/or tragedy, followed inevitably by sweet triumph.

While the angle brackets get us going, the freestanding underscore (_) plays the most important role by making visual the in-between spaces so important to Pierson's thinking. In contemporary usage the freestanding underscore most often indicates spaces in the naming of things where spaces are not allowed, like computer filenames or email addresses. For Pierson, the underscore strives to emphasize not simply a distance between related things, but rather, a key part of the experience of running that is not failure and not flow. It works akin to 間, or *Ma*, the Japanese concept commonly used to talk about negative space in art and architecture, which also denotes gaps, spaces, or intervals.

If we take the underscore as a cousin-concept to *Ma* in the space of running, we can think about the gap betwixt a runner's skin and their singlet; the space between breathes; the intervals that separate the commands 'on your marks.' 'set,' and the sound of the pistol. We can also consider the distance between first and second, and that even meaner space that separates third and fourth, the emotional expanse between standing on the podium and having your feet firmly on the ground. Most importantly, for Pierson, we can think about the threshold spaces, those exhilarating and unnerving experiences of running where the hard limit of what we thought we could do starts to go a little wiggly. This is where we can find out what we might be capable of.

This threshold space is an invisible infrastructure that runners build by running. What happens in this space can be surprising, but it cannot be fully measured. It is fleeting and difficult to describe, which is all the more reason we need to try to do so. Inside this threshold space is where we can experience ourselves in departure; this is where we can run out of our minds or make a million little failures. We feel these things before we fully know them. A threshold experience could happen during the spectacle of performance, but it could just as easily happen in training away from the razzle-dazzle of competition.

Running is at its heart a sensual practice, not a spectacular one. To run is to let space into the body, and to breathe it out; it is to eat up space with the repetitive motion of legs. There is a relationship between our movement and the ground we cover. The cadence of our little defiances of gravity can be the soundtrack to the movies in our heads where we star in exceeding quantified expectations or they can be the steady drumbeat reminding us that we are in fact tethered to the earth. Jean Baudrillard famously called the marathon a "spectacle of exhaustion." He framed running at your limit as something sad, empty, and tragic. Pierson counters this critique with his beautiful descriptions of running, where the body is set spinning, even dancing. He shows, too, that the exhaustion we desire is not to make a sorry spectacle of ourselves, instead it is to feel ourselves inside an elastic infrastructure where we can find out something new.

From inside the practice, it is not difficult to recognize that running cannot be so easily reduced to causing a scene by running yourself ragged in public. Baudrillard wasn't a runner, he didn't get it. It might seem like we crave exhaustion, and ok, we do, but more than that we are after the feeling of moving through our tiredness. When we are able to do so, we find out something from our exhaustion, and take meaning from our ability to run on that we can apply back into our running, as well as to other things in our lives. Our pain opens something up for us when we do not withdraw from it that makes space "for a passage through the limit, rather than hardening it," as French philosopher Jean-Luc Nancy writes in Corpus.[3] Sometimes the threshold space is a pain cave we learn to move around in. This is what Lauren Fleshman meant when she wrote: "That was how you won...say yes as long as possible, and then when you don't think it's possible, say yes anyway."[4] We might hit a limit, feel near death, but somehow keep going. We love it when that happens. Each time it time it does, we emerge a bit different.

Other times the running isn't so hard. Perhaps we could fly, we think, in that state of good feeling and bodily confidence that

Mihály Csíkszentmihályi called 'flow.' While the flow state has been well-theorized, Pierson asks what we can glean from the threshold space that is not quite flow and not-yet failure. Ultimately, what <Run_A_Way> shows us is that developing a philosophy of training is good but figuring out a way of training philosophy from inside the practice is better.

Notes

1. Hartmut Rosa, *Resonance: A Sociology of Our Relationship to the World*. Trans. James C. Wagner. Cambridge: Polity Press, 2019.
2. Gertrude Stein, "*On Punctuation*," in Lectures in America. Boston: Beacon Press, 1985: 214.
3. Jean-Luc Nancy, *Corpus*. Trans. Richard A. Rand. New York: Fordham University Press, 2008: 23.
4. Lauren Fleshman, *Good for a Girl: A Woman Running in a Man's World*, New York: Penguin, 2023: 165.

a running body

oscillates

between

its search for immortality

and its death by exhaustion.

by optimising its potential

to reach beyond physical limitations,

the binaries

become a threshold.

in order to go beyond

the commodification of performance,

this book will inquire into

high-intensity running as

a way

to cultivate a perceptive field.

1. RUNWAY

Spectacle of Exhaustion

they are internal and stealthy

the gates we thought

i could never

reach

near death

and eternity

i run toward them,

like a figure of speech

i remember those days,

where i encounter

new levels of pain,

it took me out of the place

and felt

like a moment of grace

where the pain was extreme,

seeing behind my glasses and closed eyes

a tunnel of black and white flashes

after a few minutes of euphoria,

i saw the light beam

i experienced death while running

i could feel my heart stopping

and my still body

maybe it's just a dead body striding

the reason i run like a madman,

is to reach these ecstatic states

through knocking at the doors of eternity

i repeatedly wish to open the gates

i want to open them all gently

between a flight and a fall

i think it is the key for the walls

raised in the empty land of sensibility

1.1. Endurance sports and the search for exhaustion

A vulnerable body

chases the horizon

without end.

What is it running after?

Maybe we could start by reversing the question:

what is it running from?

An existential quest may be found in the act of running.

as the body undergoes an unnecessary amount of effort.

The individual finds meaning in the resistance to its own fatigue.

It learns how to endure.

Fatigue becomes a way to increase one's awareness. Endurance becomes an act of resistance against the commodification of the self in daily space.

The lonely exploration of the self through its exhaustion should be revised as it is now staged and brought to a wide audience of running enthusiasts.

In current spaces and times, the isolated body becomes part of a pack.

The sport has escaped its representation as dangerous, (we can still hear athletes saying they will "run themselves to death" quite literally before a high intensity effort) perhaps reserved to a set of willing individuals, and taking space with many discriminations.[1]

As a runner may feel excited about the popularisation of the sport, we may interrogate further the existentialist pursuit of effort as it is becomes flattened in the format of global events. Let's look at the running boom through the position of a non-runner:

"I would never have believed that the (...) marathon could move you to tears. It really is the end-of-the-world show. (...) They are all seeking death, the death by exhaustion that was the fate of the first Marathon man some two thousand years ago. (...) There are too many of them and their message has lost all meaning: (...) it is a twilight message of a futile, superhuman effort. Collectively, they might rather seem to be bringing the message of a catastrophe for the human race."[2]

Jean Baudrillard probably never stood on the starting line of any running race. This "end-of-the world show" - associated with a lack of meaning, as triggered by the very common "why do you run" question - pictures a complete state of alienation of the human body into the modern competition system. Later in *America* Baudrillard, places the notion of competition as performed in sport in analogy with the competitive nature of the corporate world. It foresees a translation of the running race into one's productivity in the work environment.

What Baudrillard calls a "show" closely resembles the "specacle" of Guy Debord. In *The Society of the Spectacle*, Debord presents the "spectacle" as this hidden yet ubiquitous structure one performs in.

The democratisation of the sport results in the rise of a "leisure" running, that diminishes the existential exploration in a global dynamic. The experience of vulnerability may be revised when surrounded by thousands of exhausted bodies and cheering spectators. The individual exploration becomes systemic, as runners are striding in the same direction, Baudrillard declares that "the message has lost all meaning" to point out a form of alienation of existenticlism in physical activity. The running hype may appear as a very linear drive. Individuals show off their fatigue in the structure of "speed tunnels" both material and immaterial. Indeed, the display of races are very much limited between a start and end line, linked with a single line to follow. We may see this scene as being contradictory with a form of physical exploration, however we could also find complicity with the commodification of performance and one's capacity to displace the structures it is evolving in.

Focusing on one's experience of time, German sociologist Hartmut Rosa claims that acceleration - to be read literally, as this state of constant rush - is emblematic of late modernity and results in the alienation of mankind: the loss of the experience of time.[3] We might find more empathy for the non-running Baudrillard seeing a grotesque replica of this acceleration in a staged sport event. However, Rosa goes beyond this dead-end of alienation and brings the possibility to find its opposite (presented as resonance) through a form of complicity.

"It is very obvious that running is part of the logic of acceleration (...) it almost feels like a mode of aggression (...) and on the other hand it's maybe our form of trying to get in touch in resonance with our body (...) so that because we are so trained, so used to this mode of aggression we kind of need it to regain the sense of resonance. It's trying to gain the one through the other, trying to get in resonance through acceleration."[4]

In the age of the Anthropocene, Rosa reinterprets acceleration as a countering method. However, the current narratives argue quite literally about the way in which this search for exhaustion is rooted in the human body and how the running performance should be conducted.

We may now look at the different structural layers guiding and optimising the body towards the practice of running in order to understand how those can be used as a way to "gain the one through the other."

1.2. Crafting the performed body

Considering the scientific agreement regarding the biological evolution of "homo" as a species designed for endurance running,[1] there can be a risk of falling into a direct transposition of persistence hunting into a motivation to sign-up for a marathon race.

The act of running to survive is being glorified in plenty of running handbooks, as a way to make a few strides to feel alive. To go further, the crafting of a (running) body according to its physiological needs became a production process where many external factors interplay. However, looking at the development of the best athletes on earth, we can point to the complexity and uncertainty in one's (body) potential to reach its best level. This challenge is can be addressed through three key overreaching topics: The "performer", the "environment", and finally "practice and training".[2] Those three aspects are drawing a base picture of the elements interplaying in the (trans)formation of a body in regards to athletic practice.

In the case of elite athletes, it's clear there is an extreme conditioning that engages into the smallest details of daily life in order to make sure one's entire existence is oriented towards a performance moment.

The "performer" is stressed by its daily "practice and training" and this way it requires to shape its "environment" in a what could take the form of an ongoing performance. If this might sound as a form of search for constant exhaustion, it is important to understand the different patterns and rhythm that different runners can engage with.

The search for exhaustion becomes almost non-essential in the practice of an elite athlete. Effort instead becomes a tool to monitor performance.

In the end, a high-level athlete can be seen as the contemporary figure aiming to point at - by optimising its potential - what can a body do.[3]

The crucial difference between leisure runners and elite athletes, beyond their ambition regarding their own performance, lies in the amount of time and energy they place in the running itself. As the "performer" puts more effort in "practice and training" (which doesn't mean running harder, but running more overall), its need for recovery also increases. This way a professional athlete will invest all the non-practice moments as a potential for progression. The way one runner will adapt its "environment" appears as the most influential factor in order to understand how different approaches to running can exist.

Thus, the concept of endurance is also to be applied to a philosophy of training.

We could however share Baudrillard's vision of a "message that has lost all meaning" when looking at the democratisation of running. The intense hype around running leads to an accelerated transposition of tools and methods from the world's best athletes to the leisure runner, and furthermore, into a fashionable culture.

This phenomenon creates a bias when focusing again on running itself and how it is being experienced by different demographics. The way a body can feel a sense of ownership and control of the effort is to be found in the measurement of intensity.[4]

The feeling of exhaustion is something that the runner not only experiences physically, but also reads through an externalisation of the body into a set of data. From there, the abstract space of physical sensations becomes placed in training zones (usually based on heart-rate frequency).

This measured approach has become dominant in high-level training, but it is also becoming very accessible to a wider audience. The measurement tools found in a laboratory become accessible through commercial products.

This way, the measurement that the elite athlete uses to make sure the training remains productive becomes also an entry for the leisure runner to feel stimulated by an accessible set of data.

One's capacity to run further, faster, longer, becomes part of a crafting process that is conditioned to be measured with intensity.[4]

This reductive approach to athletes being defined by the time they run on the screens of a stadium is now popularised in the figure of someone counting their steps with their phone.

However, besides pointing how the incorporation of data into physical exercise can be beneficial to the rational understanding of physical exhaustion and its interpretation, it is curious to witness how this externalisation of the physical self into measurements can be read as a disappearance of the body as a tangible entity.

Every sport can be seen as a way to craft the body towards a specific gesture. The athlete is its own sculptor, playing with the muscles as a matter to craft with, either by addition or removal.

In the case of endurance sports, a power-weight ratio is essential, as the locomotion aspect comes into play. The body becomes a running sculpture.

However, regarding this process of optimisation and the abstraction of the physical motion into a GPS trace, it feels like there is something stealthy about the becoming of the body in running.

As it tends to get so sharp, the runner removes what is not a part of this sculpture, but in the end of this (trans)formation process, what remains?

This optimised running body is being constantly idealised through hyperbole.

2. RUN AWAY

Hyperbolic Striving

what if

my foot

never stopped

dancing

what if

my legs

never stopped

spinning

what if

my heart

never stopped

pumping

what if

my brain

didn't consider

lactates

would it be death,

or something else

maybe a state,

maybe just a faith

perhaps

what if

i could

run forever

where would i go

what space

of the earth

what rhythm

of the heart

has not been reached

yet

what if

i could

dwell without landing

what if

the flow

became

a float

facing an endless sea

where does

the absurd captain

take the body-boat

let the wind

cross the soul

from running

out of time

to running

off from time

faster, faster

this is the departure

2.1. Materialist eternity

By supposing the absence of our very physical limitations,

we may be able to project what lies behind this virtual finish line.

Running can be easily interpreted as a tragic escapist practice, where the body transports itself towards the sky and beyond, almost flying, just before getting pulled down by the magnetic field of the earth.

Supposing the removal of gravity in the reality of running, this emancipating aspect can be truly highlighted as a sort of void.[1]

Perhaps we could fly.

This sense of void resonates with the sense of lightness one feels when encountering the state of "flow".

As popularised by Mihaly Csikszentmihalyi, the flow describes this bittersweet feeling when encountering a sense of pleasure while facing a challenge.

This could be seen as yet another synonym of the "runner's high", which remains associated with the early production of endorphins after a certain moment of effort.

The necessity to grasp this very instant feeling,

as it still lays on metabolic reactions

results in a very literal representation.

The empty space becomes a metaphor for the feeling of removing oneself from the toughness of the effort.

As Nicolas Bourriaud highlights in regards to a "speculative realism"[2] the desire to break any distance with nature through a total horizontalization results in the ideal of a void, without resistance, without friction, where the flowing body finds true freedom.

The presentation of this ideal in the staged performance space may be painted as a form of trickery, likely to the illusionary aspect of the spectacle.

2.2. Spectacle of projection

The highest stage for the performed body might be seen as a form of heterotopia, brought by Foucault[1] as a utopia finding a physical situation.

When an athlete achieves a great performance, it is often mobilised in order to inspire people beyond the sport.

For instance, Nike's attempt to break a symbolic time limit on the marathon in their project *Breaking 2* (2016) entered a space of performance never reached before, by transgressing the rules of the World Athletics federation (the main concern was the rotation of pacers during that event). The reality of human performance reached a new state that used to be considered as a distant utopia.

The mechanic behind such an athletic heterotopia is pretty accessible. By removing limitation in the environmental conditions affecting a race, optimising to the highest point every details (from super-shoes to controlling the wind) despite the rules being settled, we can dress a context that brings the utopian nature of certain performances into the realm of reality. Countless world records have been beaten by amateurs running downhill, and although we know it doesn't have the same value, the existence of such times creates a confusing feeling.

The use of hyperbole is also omnipresent when talking about such performances: "Today we went to the Moon and came back to Earth" is what came out of Eliud Kipchoge's second hetertopic marathon world record attempt in Vienna. Such representations make an abstraction of the athlete becoming a distant figure, running without visible exhaustion in order to communicate a persuasive imaginary to the spectator and play with it's desire to identify and project into a challenge of its own limitation.

Expanded in space and time, we might look to the Olympic Games as such an heterotopia. Gathered around world-famous values (excellence, respect, and friendship), the world's best athletes come into a competition that is presented as an idealised humanist moment of unity through sports:

"What a sight it is to see you all parading together! What a rare and precious moment you have given us! And even though the Games cannot solve every problem, Even though discrimination and conflicts are not about to disappear, Tonight you have reminded us how beautiful humanity is when we come together. And when you return to the Olympic Village, you will be sending a message of hope to the whole world: that there is a place where people of every nationality, every culture and every religion can live together. You'll be reminding us: it is possible. For the next 16 days, you will be the best version of humanity. You'll remind us that the emotions of sport form a universal language that we all share. Until the 11th of August, we'll be by your side. Your defeats will be our defeats. Your victories will be our victories. Your emotions… will be our emotions."[2]

The message of hope and the inspirational aspect of high performance shall not be denied. However it is also clear that the modern Olympics are a show that is not detached from conflicts between nations. Indeed, athletes are performing under the entire world's cameras while representing their country. They live for two weeks in an Olympic village, the materialisation of a utopian peace brought by the playfulness of sports. We could also point out how the major sport brands logos sit right next to national flags on the racing kits, placing the very corporate competition discussed earlier along with the direct competition of nations in an event that aims for unity.

In order to deconstruct this very structured search for togetherness, we can look at the experience of a running pack, and balance the critique of competition as another method of aggression that could be valued as a way to enter in resonance, in this scale, with other individuals.

The Olympic games are inherently a competition event. Even in the individual sport, the spectacle finds its value in the comparison of an athlete's physical "excellence" in regards to other's. Adversity is a very direct way to reach beyond one's own limitations, as experienced in a *peloton*. Beyond the science of drafting – aiming to lower the resistance of air by evolving in a sort of human tunnel – the runner finds mental stimulation in the presence of others as a direct direction to move along with.

The opposition system in middle-distance running is a way to drive the body against the raw effort pursued while embracing its condition as a social creature. As mentioned by Bernard Stiegler in *Acting Out*, "This sociality is the framework of a becoming: the group, and the individual in that group, ever cease to seek out their path."

Stiegler insists on the rooted aspect of this collective quest, while also acknowledging its specific experience: "This search *constitutes* human time. And if the time of the *I* is certainly not the time of the *we*, it takes place within the time of the *we* which is itself conditioned by the time of the *I*'s of which it is composed".[3] This collective sense of effort brings a better understanding of the experience of a competitive nature as performed during the very intense context of a competition. The complicity between aggression and resonance (Rosa) finds its first root in the experience of other bodies. Perhaps the *peloton* could be seen as a vehicle for the athlete to perform in regards to a "form" of transindividuation. In their book *Towards a Transindividual Self – A Study in Social Dramaturgy*, Bojana Cvejić, and Ana Vujanović are reflecting back on Simondon's thoughts on individuation[4] beyond the individual and the way it performs itself, presented as "incomplete in relation to another individual."[5] Opposition in sport should be read as a constitutive part of the transcendental ideal in performance. From there the values of "respect" and "friendship" brings this structure at the scale of an ideal of cohabitation.

In the rushed motion of a race, one can find its place in the world by experiencing the existence of others. I can feel the exhaustion of my opponents, hence it also affects my perceptive field while I as a subject disappear: the individual blends and emerges among the peloton.

The sculptural practice is shifting from the individual weight/power ratio to engage in the aesthetic of transindividuality. The representational aspect comes into play in the staging of a race, as the athlete gets not only to be doing, but rather showing doing. Perhaps the pursue of performance in running could be compared to artistic sports like ballet, where the body's gesture becomes a matter of a rehearsed choreography transgressing pain in motion.

The material conditions of a race are supposed to optimise the pursuit for effort, by offering a very direct dynamic as pictured by the standardised figure of the running track. The lanes to loop in between of as well as the sum of material and immaterial agents (crowd cheering, pistol) appear as a sum of scores for the body to perform the running piece. The interplay with the adrenaline build-up following the projection of the individual into its performance will also be developed in the last section in regards to the notion of virtuality.

However, we can acknowledge here how the competition context seems to rely mostly on a very external conditioning process. The design of a running race appears as an attempt to stimulate artificially transindividuation of the body in the *peloton*. The race builds an immaterial dynamic engaging the body in the "speed tunnel" where its individual self disappears in the rhythm of its stride.

This search of propelled performance finds its expression in a sort of replica, or rather a search for augmentation of the base structure of the peloton. For instance, the introduction of the Wavelight technology - a set of LED lights placed on the inside of the track and guiding the athletes following a programmed pace - brings a sense of control and ownership on the very abstract notion of speed. The measurement system where the body becomes externalised as a rational set of data invests not only the trace, as compared to the documentation of an art-performance, but it becomes part of the piece itself taking the form of a pacer made not of flesh but of light.

Technology, presented as a way to increase one's potential triggers the nature of the effort itself, by slowly detaching the athlete from the physicality of the performance.

2.3. On the augmented body

With every innovation brought into a sport, the question is to measure the line between the rewarding contribution obtained and the alienating aspect that can be found when a technology substitutes the body at work. In the situation of athletics, the most evident topic to discuss the impact of technology in human performance is the innovations placed in running shoes.

The ideal of lightness that existed in the design of racing shoes got replaced by carbon plates sandwiched between highly responsive foams. The benefits of this addition between the body and the ground are so important, as the athlete increases its running economy (extra energy return optimising muscular energy consumption), that the last years of athletic performances have been shaken by world records in an overwhelming frequency. Perhaps the World Athletic federation has been busy trying to regulate the use of such a technology, limiting the amount of foam (measured on the heel) to a rather fixed value.[1] The term "technological doping" has been used to compare the introduction of carbon-plated shoes in the early 2020's with the banned swimming suits that increased hydrodynamic ten years prior to that. The notion of doping is used to condemn the artificiality of performances using external tools to increase physical capacities.

However, unlike the use of banned substances for instance, the running shoes remain an external and detachable prosthesis. It may not affect directly the physical health of the body, however, we could tackle the specificity of those racing shoes, as they are initially designed to "function" at a certain speed – it requires a certain pressure and a right amount of weight to get a proper effect from the stiffness of the carbon plate. Introduced to a wider audience as a shoe to boost your performance, the impact it has on the running stride should not be denied, as it may tend to replace the natural elasticity of the tendons and the reactivity of the foot itself. If the swimming suit has been banned as the gap generated on world performance was far more important compared to the carbon shoes, we can wonder what is the fundamental difference regarding the ethics of sport that made those remain "legal".

The context behind the introduction of a technology will have an effect on its reception. Perhaps, we may speculate that the effect of new racing shoes felt more smooth than the case of a swimsuit – in order to understand its acceptance by the federation. The specificity of every sport's rule also comes into play in order to introduce regulation in regards to a new technology.

This search of augmentation triggers an ethic that is very unique to the sport, however it stresses a common interrogation regarding the very linear transposition of those technologies into the daily realm. As mentioned earlier, countless external factors are involved when looking at the making of an athlete. But the immediate commercialisation of those super-shoes may relate with the earlier critique of an ubiquitous spectacle. The existentialist stride characterised by the expression of exhaustion is lost, leaving only a super-human to perform this "end of the world show" mentioned by Baudrillard. Indeed, the problem with this literality in performance is that the search for optimisation in the case of the high-level athlete tends to a form of substitution for the amateur.

To phrase it differently, the quest of physiological progress is replaced by an equipment hunt. Technology becomes a stepping-stone against exhaustion, and the act of running becomes mediated by this artificial conditioning solely, in spite of physicality.

"Augmented man remains a dream product that is consumed in the Olympic stadium once every four years."[2]

This substitution of capacities resonates outside of the stadium. Seeking a sense of limitlessness, the augmented human is perhaps the result of a *run_away* from the tragic condition of the body, being attached to Earth as a mortal entity.

This interpretation, however, portrays a body distant from everything, including perception. Perhaps this transhuman state, as an attempt to escape death, can also be understood as the death of the body. The over-equipped body loses track off the soil, and the act of flowing becomes deprived of any physicality.

The figure of the athlete as a "prosthetic God"[3] questions the very thin line where the augmentation of oneself becomes a deadly substitution. In Mamoru Oshii's 1995 adaptation of *Ghost in the Shell*, the iconic boat scene stages a reflection on the individuation of one-self as a machine. In spite of being self-conditioned as a cyborg, Major Motoko Kusanagi interrogates on destiny in a vulnerable way regarding what remains of the body and one's capacity to explore its physical potential:

"There are countless ingredients that make up the human body and mind, like all the components that make up me as an individual with my own personality. Sure I have a face and voice to distinguish myself from others, but my thoughts and memories are unique only to me, and I carry a sense of my own destiny. Each of those things are just a small part of it. I collect information to use in my own way. All of that blends to create a mixture that forms me and gives rise to my conscience. I feel confined, only free to expand myself within boundaries."[4]

The concept of cyborg as found in the *Cyborg Manifesto* by Donna J. Haraway may help us to understand the complicity between this form of destiny for machines and a sense of resonance beyond the risk of alienation as also discussed by Rosa.

"Individuation and gender formation, depend[s] on the plot of original unity out of which difference must be produced and enlisted in a drama of escalating domination of woman/nature. The cyborg skips the step of original unity, of identification with nature in the Western sense."[5]

If the never-landing body, distant from everything even the technological assistance that made it achieve immortality appears as a deadly end, we are forced to acknowledge the presence of external forces in the process of transindividuation. Perhaps, in an attempt to understand the experience of the self beyond rigid boundaries, we may look into the cyborg as a way to grasp what constitutes a being in a more fluid way. The cyborg is in-between, yet not unrooted. As pictured in running, the boundaries of the accelerated body become harder to grasp. Perhaps we might invest this in-between state, the temporary unattached and ineffable body oscillating in suspension during its stride.

The act of running may be a physical demonstration, a performance of the body dwelling in a threshold state, and experiencing its relation with a perceptive field through not complete detachment, but a critical distance.

3. RUN A WAY

Dwelling in the Threshold

what is a track

this display of lines

breaking a landscape

they settle in this very dimension

flat against the void

i elevate by looping around

in a non-grounded track

the lap is up there

in the lost space

i feel it,

a sensation

it cannot be constructed

i land again

on the raw mondotrack

energy floating around

i feel like dancing

i get on the stage

i enter the projectors

become the illusion

and disappear

become a trace

humidity in the air

a concentration of energy

a bright focus

the peloton

becomes a planet

the trace of running

lies in this dimension

i embrace the machine

stillness in motion

i was amazed

the sole of my foot

became dusty and bright

just like the road i took

3.1. In search of the lost sensation

The world of the sensation remains a central drive in the athlete's perception of its effort. In the end of a practice or race, we can hear many athletes saying their sensation was either good or bad.

We shall perhaps open up this section by dissecting the mechanics behind the objectification of such an ineffable phenomenon.

We could see running as way (among many other activities) to stimulate one's awareness towards it's physical feelings.

The sum of heart rate getting higher, capillaries and muscles adapting to the intensity of the effort doesn't leave the conscious self unharmed. The base principle of endurance is indeed to not only optimise the body's potential, nor to learn how to fight against the exhaustion. At some point, the ongoing performance of running is about an individual embracing it's "sensation" either in pleasure or pain, and becoming one with its body and its stride.

In the *Phenomenology of Perception*,[1] Maurice Merleau-Ponty highlights the capacity of the individual to project itself from the body. Merleau-Ponty's take on sensation as a relational structure between the body and its environment comes with the composition of a set of "clean objects" – in the Platonic pure and absolute way – from which the body can navigate towards.

We may look at rational structures – from orthonormality to the lines of the running track – as such representative guides to navigate the blindfolded space of sensation.

This phenomenological approach allows us to place the body as central in the process of feeling, however when placed in motion, this very self-centred viewpoint becomes less linear. Investing the void between two perceptive points leads beyond a dualist conception of the body and the act of positioning in space. Movement allows oneself to access perspective, or, a critical distance.

Looking back at the quest of disappearance, we could strive towards an understanding of the world through the measure of the body[2] and how this takes the form of an individual both emerging and blending from the structure it is running in.

Before diving into the pre-conscious self and how it can be reached in practice, we may look at the initial projection of the world through a very mental yet tangible state[3], the virtual.

3.2. Virtuality as a state

The phenomenological access to "sensation" can be situated in the performer's body as it is undergoing a certain stress. When engaging in a very repetitive activity – such as running – the physical gesture enters a realm of incorporation.

Repetition becomes a method to understand the making of virtuosity.

At some point in the exercise "consciousness lets go."[1]

When looking at the highest performers in their fields, it feels like the movement becomes operated without the direct order of the consciousness in their own body.

"The body acquires a *tekne* about its own capacity."[2]

"Imagine a young pianist just about to enter the stage in order to perform Brahms' piano concerto nr. 2 in b flat major, op. 83. The performance will start in a few minutes, the musicians of the orchestra are already seated in their playing positions, the conductor will soon touch her shoulders as a sign to go on stage, and our soloist's mind is probably fully concentrated on the first two pages of the score, on the piano's dialogue with the horns, followed by the daunting cadence which leads to the entry of the full orchestra. In this particular moment, in the very last seconds before going on stage, the whole concerto—all its pitches, rhythms, overall form, instrumental colours, dynamic ranges, tempi, pedalling, fingerings, gestures—all those things are vividly present in the pianist's body and mind, being concretely felt as a huge field of virtuality. A virtual that is not to be understood in terms of virtual reality, but, on the contrary, as something absolutely real, something that exists and that is perceived in this very moment—just before starting the performance—as tension, as an infinite reservoir of possible actualisations, some of which will happen, and which will start happening as soon as the conductor beats the first bar."[3]

The Deleuzian conception of the virtual differs from the modern reading of the word, as associated with virtual reality. However, as this illusionary and constructed space can be an analogy of the spectacle stages, it feels relevant to see how it can be stressed in regards to the very physical perception of the virtual.

The ideal of an empty space remains in both conceptions, however the projection dynamics are expressed in quite different ways.

As the virtual reality offers the illusion of an escape through a replication of reality, the physical body invests the virtual rather as the space where it can experience this sense of limitlessness without being detached from its condition.

In the end, virtuality could be understood as the grey zone where the real overlaps with either a fictional or a projected world. The border between the individual and the player dissolves, and the body now stands on an edge, perhaps a threshold.

The gun is about to go off. The race is about to start. The body is stressed between its own death and an elevated state of life. Let's finally dive into this threshold.

3.3. Never really a departure

"I felt that I simply touched the closed shell of a being, that, from within, had accessed to infinity."[1]

The running space - and its idealisation in the form of a heterotopia - is not detached from reality. The escapist approach to running supposes the pre-existence of limiting structures pictured as the alienating grids of modernity - from which the heroic figure of the athlete manages to run away. The search for exhaustion becomes captured in inspiring narratives where the virtual and its potential becomes an instrument to create a relation and a sense of ownership of flow.

The Spinozist exploration in athletic pursuit becomes a direct way to inspire individuals to strive for the best version of themselves.[2] This literal approach results in the diminution of one's own potential.

It may feel more relevant however to shift the focus from the virtual replicas of finish-lines to the actual state where running is experienced and how the body engages with it. The simple reason behind this gesture is to be found in the unpredictability of the conditions that pre-exist the performance. Even when trying to monitor them, the sum of external elements interfering in the making of performance (not to mention that the body is also never in the same "race" shape), one may not be able to reproduce the same race twice.

After all, there is no starting line.

After looking at the embodied knowledge and the presence of virtuality in the practice, that is already run into the body, we may indeed declare that the physical starting line is actually not the start of the run.

Although running may be a repetitive sport, and the act of "looping" could be compared with Nietzsche's concept of eternal recurrence, the resonance found in movement and the way we could approach this relation can be expressed more clearly in Heraclitus's formula: "No man ever steps in the same river twice. For it's not the same river and he's not the same man." This idea of constant transformation allows us to approach the ineffable nature of running. Perhaps we may look at the running body as a material that is constantly produced in the realm of virtuality, in this in-between state.

This dynamic condition may not be understood as detached from the virtual points it is oscillating within, but rather as dwelling in this void. By shifting from the eternal loop of frustration, aspiring for constant motion while trying to escape exhaustion itself, the threshold reveals itself to be the space where the body can explore its true potential. The body may be looping in the void, but this pursuit of endurance may be indeed presented as an act of revolt[3] against the commodification of life.

We may now be approaching *Ma*. This concept, which is difficult to translate from Japanese, has been used to describe the interplay with negative space, also compared through the words intervals, gap, or threshold. Its interpretation may be found in various domains, ranging from the space between the skin and the kimono as well as the attention to empty space in architecture or music. The complexity of *Ma* for the West lies in the concept's unity between both time and space:

"Ma is a structural unit of a living space.
(...)
Originally the concept of Ma had represented the distance between the two points; it later began to indicate a space surrounded by walls on four sides, and then eventually it meant a room. As one might guess from the process in which the word gained broader meanings in history, a "living space" once was no more than an empty space with no surrounding walls but with only pôles erected at its four corners.
(...)
Thus even space is transient: it fades, leaving behind the branches of time."[4]

Perhaps we may understand *Ma* as a way "to inhabit the everyday life (...) in a state of stupor."[5] The phenomenological approach highlights how the body navigates the world from within. My proposal is to speculate the existence of *Ma* not as a construct, but through personification, making *Ma* a transindiviudal character: a force that lays in the virtual, as the result of the individual blending and emerging from the running performance.

This gesture aims to emancipate the escapist representation of running (expressed through the abstraction of elite athletes into worship figures), and the next step will be to investigate how the performative nature of this character can be activated against the commodification of life as staged in stadiums.

"Research has to go through a body; it has to be lived in some sense—transformed into some sort of lived experience—in order to become whatever we might call art. (...) A lot of art now just points at things. Merely the transfer of something into a gallery is enough to bracket it as art."[6]

How can this approach to *Ma* can be conducted and staged in the context of elite performance? We move from the runaway to the *run_a_way.*

3.4. Athle_tics in motion

How to approach the ineffability of the threshold?

We may look at *Ma* as a pretty furtive figure, in analogy to the novel from Alain Damasio.[1] In this futuristic dystopia, "the stealthies" are presented as a figure full of hope and power (in the Spinozist understanding as "potentia") resisting the ubiquitous process of tracking and the way the body undergoes a reduction of its potential when evolving in what Damasio calls "techno-cocoons". This stealthy approach values invisible sensation in spite of the visual and rational perception.

The careful gesture towards a state that dwells in the last bits of emptiness can be compared to the choreography of the characters in Andrei Tarkovsky's "Stalker" (1979). The three protagonists evolve in different scenes under the direction of the "Stalker" (played by Alexander Kaidanovsky). Tarkovsky transfigures what may appear as empty fields and abandoned factories into a (virtual) space full of potentiality. The bodies' full of stupor and fear gestures towards "the Zone" showcases how the stride in the virtual can be performed beyond figuration. Tarkovsky uses the fog as an activator to make the viewer feel a transition into a reality where the usual aesthetics codes of representation are replaced by the experience of the sublime.

When looking back at the the sensation of exhaustion, we might understand how this phenomenological body can be approached aesthetically, as something exceeding the rational realm of perception:

"What is terrible – or sublime – for Kant, in his Analytic of the Sublime of 1790, is formlessness. Beauty, so say the Kantian aestheticians, has form. Its objects have definable 'boundaries, while the sublime 'is to be found in a formless object, that is to say, an object that suggests 'boundlessness', an object without end. Wild, eruptive nature – the swirling sea, massive ice floes, a looming, dark, snow-capped mountain, a churning ice storm, a sudden chasm – provokes in the viewer a welter of feelings, most notably a type of terror as the mind realises the immensity and indifference to humanity of that which is perceived. Friedrich's jagged ice pile and frozen sea is a representation of such a formless muddle, unbounded in its perversion of what might seem to be the natural order? According to the theory of the sublime the mind struggles to regain its composure and its superiority to this blind nature. As a result of this struggle with bound-lessness, that which we cannot imagine or represent adequately should, according to Kant, ultimately be contained mentally, that is, bounded within thought, within Reason. The sublime experience asserts finally a conceptual victory over blind, formless nature. The catastrophe is contained conceptually. An immense totality is encapsulated in a tiny mind."[2]

In an attempt to go beyond the romantic and detached conception of sublimity as understood in the Kantian reason, I want to understand how this "mechanic of the sublime", to be found in this admiration of fear, can be experienced physically. The running performance is a very straightforward way to experience vulnerability the search for exhaustion can be situated in the realm of a sublime aesthetic with regards to the state of constant change mentioned before.

The body runs towards its own shadow as an attempt to dwell in the "fluid" form of its movement.

We could compare running with butoh in the way both practices explore and perform the "darkness" of the body (the "show of exhaustion" according to Baudrillard). Butoh dance stages a body that has been crossed by a lightning bolt "piercing the mask"[3] of the self. Thus it is turned into an empty shell, able to apprehend its surroundings without the usual boundaries of perception.

Perhaps running, in the way it stimulates the body in exhaustion and repetition, can pave the way towards the culture of a perceptive field, that is not to be found outside of the body but within its very physical sense of boundaries.

If we consider athletics as a way to craft the body, this furtive approach to *Ma* rather presents an attempt not to sculpt the body, but understand how this ineffable (from it's essence being to be a constant movement) entity may be questioning the limits of materiality. Beyond the development of a perceptive field, how can running performance operate not as a rejection but as a displacement of the commodified structures the body evolves within?

We may encounter Simondon's "liberation by technique"[4] when extending the way the self finds resonance in aggression in the running pack to the case of technical objects. In the end, the cyborg finds complicity with the augmented human as it is situated in a pre-conscious state. The idea behind this desire of reappropriating the world can be found in the International Situationist movement,[5] using the score of the "derive", a liberated wonder in the grids of the city resulting in the creation of "psychogeographic maps". Beyond trying to challenge the representation of the self in the world, I aim to invest the linearity found in memory and the way we apprehend the world and run through this variety of objects. *Ma* presents itself as this empty shell that interacts (from its essence as a cyborg) with its surrounding in this state of constant stupor. From there, the process of liberating the self from the dualist tension - as found in the virtuality of running - can become a method to reconsider the cultural techniques that pre-exist any mode of being.

"When I inherit an object, a flint-cutting tool, I inherit through its mode of use, that is, the gestures, the motor behaviours that lead to the production of flint-cutting tools. With the appearance of technical objects, a new stratum of memory is constituted, which permits the transmission from generation to generation of individual experience and permits mutualisation in the form of what we call a we."[6]

This transindividual materiality dwells in the performer's body, and we can understand this process of displacement as a way to go beyond the conformity of function and perhaps develop a design practice in the empty space of the virtual.

"With a wall all around .
A clay bowl is molded;
But the use of the bowl .
Will depend on the part.
Of the bowl that is void.

Cut out windows and doors
In the house that you build;
But the use of the house
Will depend on the part
Of the house that is void."[7]

Focusing on the performing character(s) of *run[ning]_a_way* aims to exploring the potential of the sport and open-up transformation(s) of the performance stage.

3.5. Playing with_in the threshold

In the series of *Drawing Restrained*, Matthew Barney challenges the experience of the body in sport, as the athlete undergoes a set of physical restrictions (the rules of a sport) in order to explore it as scores from which to record the physical gesture. Barney claims:

"The athlete is the artist."[1]

We may not however over-interpret the body's potential to reach this state. As we discussed earlier, the making of an athlete is a very exhaustive process engaging a variety of conditions. The transindividuation towards *Ma* shall not fall in the trap of becoming a method, as this occurs in running handbooks, taking ownership of the "sensation" to pave a linear way to train along with. How to bring the furtiveness of running outside of running, by running?

We may not ignore the differences between the experience of an elite athlete and the figure of the "amateur" (Stiegler). Although running remains running, regardless of measurements, we might want to acknowledge the metabolic perceptions that comes into play, when seeking exhaustion beyond the tools used to measure them (lactate machine, heart-rate monitor).

We might look at the externalisation of intensity – in the context of a lab testing as a peak experience of the body exploring sensation while acknowledging its relation with surrounding techniques. Perhaps the sublime in *athle_tics* may be found in the overreaching of this augmented self through intensity itself. In the "situation" of a lab testing, the relation with the complex sets of data overlaps with the body reaching a state of effort where he can no longer interpret them.

Indeterminacy – this state of not being measured[2] – is a perfect example of this interplay in the threshold between technology and sensation. The measured reading of threshold(s), as an essential tool for the athlete to situate training zones, should be re-interpreted beyond the commodified experience of a running watch.

By focusing on this playful aspect regarding exhaustion, we might be able to expand the experience of running beyond the structures of sport. Johan Huizinga claims in *Homo Ludens* the existential nature of playing:

"In play there is something 'at play' which transcends the immediate needs of life and imparts meaning to the action. All play means something. If we call the active principle that makes up the essence of play, "instinct", we explain nothing; if we call it "mind" or "will" we say too much. However we may regard it, the very fact that play has a meaning implies a non-materialistic quality in the nature of the thing itself."[3]

We might head towards this complicit game between physical and physiological limitations and how it can be trained in a playful format with external elements.

The condition for the athlete to perform becomes the constraints from which it can design from.

We may find complicity with the very direct performative goal in the sport of running to play between the lines of numbers to explore the phenomelogical experience that they tend to substitute.

In the end, maybe I could break the distance between the performer and the witness of the performance. How to engage oneself into the sensation of sublime exhaustion?
Run_a_way towards playable destiny.

"The knowledge of our body is the result of a continuous effort. (...) The development is guided by experience, trial and error, effort and attempt. Only in such a way we can gain the organised knowledge of our body".[4]

\<finish\>

colourful atmosphere

body in a trance

running like a dance

take off

and settle in the flare

Footnotes

1.1. ENDURANCE SPORTS AND THE SEARCH FOR EXHAUSTION

[^1]: The case of Kathrine Switzer, the first woman to complete an official marathon while being chased by the organisation to stop her feels pretty outdated.

[^2]: Baudrillard, Jean. *Amérique*. Lgf. 1988. p.19.

[^3]: Rosa, Hartmut. *Aliénation et accélération - Vers une théorie critique de la modernité tardive*. La découverte. 2014.

[^4]: Rosa, Hartmut. "Resonnance and alienation. Two modes of experiencing time?" 2019. https://www.youtube.com/watch?v=57hqmqyQfdk

1.2. CRAFTING THE PERFORMED BODY

[^1]: Bramble, Dennis M. Lieberman, Daniel E. "Endurance running and the evolution of 'Homo'". *Nature* 432. 2004. p.345–352. doi.org/10.1038/nature03052

[^2]: Rees, Tim and: Abernethy, Bruce. Côté, Jean. Güllich, Arne. Hardy, Lew. Laing, Stewart. Montgomery, Hugh. Warr, Chelsea. Woodman, Tim. "The Great British Medalists Project: A Review of Current Knowledge on the Development of the World's Best Sporting Talent." _Sports Med_ 46, 1041–1058 (2016). https://doi.org/10.1007/s40279-016-0476-2

[^3]: "The spinozist 'scream': what can a body do?" *The Funambulist*. Edited by Léopold Lambert. 2013. thefunambulist.net/editorials/spinoza-episode-5-the-spinozist-scream-what-can-a-body-do#top

[^4]: Seiler, Stephen. "How 'normal people' can train like the worlds best endurance athletes". 2019. youtube.com/watch?v=MALsI0mJ09I

2.1. MATERIALIST ETERNITY

[^1]: Megaforce agency for Burberry. *Open spaces.* 2022. youtube.com/watch?v=pIgDRxkuwwg

[^2]: Bourriaud, Nicolas. Zhong Mengual, Estelle. "S'inspirer, respirer – Ce que le vivant fait à l'art." 2021. youtube.com/watch?v=ywnKfUwBo7I

2.2. SPECTACLE OF PROJECTION

[^1]: Foucault, Michel. *Of Other Spaces*. Published in *Architecture /Mouvement/ Continuité*. 1984 foucault.info/documents/heterotopia/foucault.heteroTopia.en/

[^2]: Estanguet, Tony. Official speech delivered at the Opening Ceremony of the Paris 2024 Olympic Games. presse.paris2024.org/actualites/discours-officiel-de-tony-estanguet-prononce-lors-de-la-ceremonie-douverture-des-jeux-olympiques-de-paris-2024-90382-e0190.html

[^3]: Stiegler, Bernard. Acting Out. Stanford University Press. 2009.

[^4]: Simondon, Gilbert. *Individuation à la lumière des notions de forme et d'informations*. Millon Jerome Eds. 2005.

[^5]: Cvejić, Bojana. Vujanović, Ana. *Toward a Transindividual Self - A Study in Social Dramaturgy*. Oslo National Academy of the Arts. Brussels. 2022.

2.3. ON THE AUGMENTED BODY

[^1]: We can highlight the subjective value of the regulation applied, as the World Athletic (https://certcheck.worldathletics.orgshoe-list) introduced in 2021 still evolved after the Paris 2024 Olympics.

[^2]: Van der Bossche, Anthony. Cited in: Rubini, Constance. *Biennale internationale Design 2006 Saint-Etienne*. Cité du design. 2006. p.56. (Personal translation).

[^3]: *The Prosthetic Impulse - From a Posthuman Present to a Biocultural Future*. Edited by Marquard Smith and Joanne Morra. MIT Press. 2006.

[^4]: Oshii, Mamoru. "Ghost in the Shell Boat Scene." From 1995 film. youtube.com/watch?v=ryJSu1f8Hi4

[^5]: Haraway, Donna. *A Cyborg Manifesto*. University of Minnesota Press, 2016.

3.1. THE SEARCH OF THE LOST SENSATION

[^1]: Merleau-Ponty, Maurice. *Phénoménologie de la perception.* Gallimard. 1945.

[^2]: Rekow-Fond, Lydie. "Rendre le monde à sa mesure- Corps et perception de l'espace." *Érudit - Sens Public - Corps contemporain et espace vécu.* 2017 erudit.org/fr/revues/sp/2017-sp03802/1048852ar/

[^3]: The word state here refers both to a physical experience as well as how it can be perceived spacewise.

3.2. VIRTUALITY AS A STATE

[^1]: De Assis. Paolo. *Gilbert Simondon's 'Transduction' as Radical Immanence in Performance*. Performance Philosophy. 2017. performancephilosophy.org/journal/article/view/140

[^2]: Bergson, Henri. *La pensée et le mouvant*. Puf, Quadrige. 2013. Quotation from: RadioFrance - *Les chemins de la philosophie - Philosophie des arts martiaux - Episode 2/4 : Judo, karaté, aïkido : comment suivre la Voie ?* 2021. radiofrance.fr/franceculture/podcasts/les-chemins-de-la-philosophie/judo-karate-aikido-comment-suivre-la-voie-9475163

[^3]: Cvejić, Bojana. Vujanović, Ana. *Toward a Transindividual Self - A Study in Social Dramaturgy*. Oslo National Academy of the Arts. Brussels. 2022.

3.3. NEVER REALLY A DEPARTURE

[^1]: Bataille, Georges. *L'expérience intérieure*. Gallimard, 1978. p.131.132. (Personal translation).

[^2]: We can look at the commercial formula: "If you have a body, you are an athlete" as an example of this very linear investment of potentiality. Nike. *After all, there is No Finish Line*. Actual Source. 2023.

[^3]: Camus, Albert. *L'Homme révolté*. Gallimard. Mai 1985.

[^4]: Izozaki, Arata. *Ma - Espace/Temps au japon - Document de communication du Festival d'Automne à Paris*. Musée des Arts Décoratifs. 1978.

[^5]: Leslie, Esther. *Liquid Crystals - The Science and Art of a Fluid Form*. Reaktion Books. 2016

[^6]: Mark Leckey in conversation with Mark Fisher. "Art Stigmergy". *Kaleidoscope Almanac of Contemporary Aesthetics*, no. 11 (Summer 2011). kaleidoscope.media/article/mark-leckey

3.4. ATHLE_TICS IN MOTION

[^1]: Damasio, Alain. *Les furtifs*. Gallimard. 2021.

[^2]: Leslie, Esther. *Liquid Crystals – The Science and Art of a Fluid Form*. Reaktion Books. 2016

[^3]: Moore, Richard. Butoh – Piercing the Mask: Abandonment of the Self. 1991. Extract from the documentary: youtube.com/watch?v=a0_WlmDUSRk

[^4]: Simondon, Gilbert. *Du mode d'existence des objets techniques*. Aubier. 2012.

[^5]: Marcolini, Patrick. *Le mouvement situationniste – Une histoire intellectuelle*. L'Echappée. 2012.

[^6]: Stiegler, Bernard. Acting Out. Stanford University Press. 2009.

[^7]: Tzu, Lao. *Tao Te Ching – XI*. Translated by Raymond B. Blakney. 1995. terebess.hu/english/tao/blakney.html

3.5. PLAYING WITH_IN THE THRESHOLD

[^1]: Frangi, Simone. "The athlete is the artist, the artist is the athlete - A reading of Matthew Barney's Hypertrophy." 2012. rheinsprung11.unibas.ch/fileadmin/documents/Edition_PDF/Ausgabe03/vor-einem-bild.pdf

[^2]: As defnied by Desiree Foester, see *Aesthetic Experience of Processes*. 2020. dfoerster1.wixsite.com/dissertation

[^3]: Huizinga, Johan. *Homo Ludens - Essai sur la fonction sociale du jeu*. Gallimard. 1976. (Personal translation).

[^4]: Paul Schilder, The image and appearance of the human body. Cited in: Frangi, Simone. "The athlete is the artist, the artist is the athlete - A reading of Matthew Barney's Hypertrophy." 2012. rheinsprung11.unibas.ch/fileadmin/documents/Edition_PDF/Ausgabe03/vor-einem-bild.pdf

Other materials

PUBLICATIONS

A. Freeman, Lyndsey. *Running*. Duke University Press. *Practices*. 2023.

Artaud, Antonin. *Le théâtre et son double*. Gallimard. 1985.

Bachelard, Gaston. *La poétique de l'espace*. Puf, *Quadrige*. 2020.

Bale, John. *Running Cultures – Racing in Time and Space*. Routledge. 2004.

Basar, Shumon. Coupland, Douglas. Ulrich Obist, Hans. *The Extreme Self*. Walther König. 2021.

Bataille, Georges. *L'expérience intérieure*. Gallimard, 1978.

Baudrillard, Jean. *Amérique*. Lgf. 1988.

Bergson, Henri. *La pensée et le mouvant*. Puf, *Quadrige*. 2013.

Bishop, Claire. *Disordered Attention - How We Look at Art and Performance Today*. Verso Books. 2024.

Campbell, Joseph. *The Hero with a Thousand Faces*. New World Library. 2008.

Camus, Albert. *L'Étranger*. Gallimard. January 1972.
Camus, Albert. *Le mythe de Sisyphe*. Gallimard. February 1985.
Camus, Albert. *L'Homme révolté*. Gallimard. Mai 1985.

Coher, Sylvain. *Vaincre à Rome*. Actes Sud. 2019.

Cvejić, Bojana. Vujanović, Ana. *Toward a Transindividual Self – A Study in Social Dramaturgy*. Oslo National Academy of the Arts. Brussels. 2022.

Damasio, Alain. *Les furtifs*. Gallimard. 2021.

Didi-Huberman, Georges. *L'Homme qui marchait dans la couleur*. Les Editions de Minuit. 2001.

Desnos, Robert. *Corps et biens*. Gallimard. 1968.

Flusser, Vilém. *Choses et non-choses – Esquisses phénoménologiques*. Editions Jacqueline Chambon. 1996.
Flusser, Vilém. *Petite philosophie du design*. Translated by Claude Maillard. Circé. 2002.

Global Tools – When Education Coincides with Life – 1973–1975. Edited by Valerio Borgonuovo and Silvia Franceschini. Les presses du réel. 2022.

Huizinga, Johan. *Homo Ludens – Essai sur la fonction sociale du jeu*. Gallimard. 1976.

Jane Norman, Sally. "Cette balançoire, chose qui me dessine, qui m'attire". *Le Comportement des Choses*. Edited by Emanuele Quinz. Translated by Lise Thiollier. Presses universitaires de Paris Nanterre. 2021. p.256-257.

J. Haraway, Donna. *A Cyborg Manifesto*. University of Minnesota Press, 2016

Kaur, Rupi. *Home Body*. Translated by Sabine Rolland. Pocket. 2022.

Leslie, Esther. *Liquid Crystals – The Science and Art of a Fluid Form*. Reaktion Books. 2016

Mauss, Marcel. *Les techniques du corps*. Flammarion. 2023.

Maulpoix, Jean-Michel. *La véritable demeure du poète est sa solitude* - in *Habiter poétiquement le monde*. Poesis. 2016. p.379.

Merleau-Ponty, Maurice. *Phénoménologie de la perception*. Gallimard. 1945.

Nike. *After all, there is No Finish Line*. Actual Source. 2023.

Rosa, Hartmut. *Aliénation et accélération - Vers une théorie critique de la modernité tardive*. La découverte. 2014.

Teiji, Itō. *La beauté du seuil - Esthétique japonaise de la limite*. Directed and translated by Philippr Bonnin. Cnrs Editions. 2021.

The Prosthetic Impulse - From a Posthuman Present to a Biocultural Future. Edited by Marquard Smith and Joanne Morra. MIT Press. 2006.

Simondon, Gilbert. *Du mode d'existence des objets techniques*. Aubier. 2012.
Simondon, Gilbert. *Individuation à la lumière des notions de forme et d'informations*. Millon Jerome Eds. 2005.

Van der Bossche, Anthony. Cited in: Rubini, Constance. *Biennale internationale Design 2006 Saint-Etienne*. Cité du design. 2006. p.56.

Weil, Simone. *La pesanteur et la grâce*. Pocket. 1991.

ARTICLES

'Athlétisme', online definition according to Wikipedia. fr.wikipedia.org/wiki/Athlétisme

Berrod, Léa-Trâm. "'Butoh', the Revolutionary Dance of Shadows." pen-online.com/arts/butoh-the-revolutionary-dance-of-shadows/?scrolled=0. 2023

Bramble, Dennis M. Lieberman, Daniel E. "Endurance running and the evolution of 'Homo'". *Nature* 432. 2004. p.345–352. doi.org/10.1038/nature03052

Bluemink, Matt. "On Virtuality: Deleuze, Bergson, Simondon.' *Epoché* Issue 36. December 2020. epochemagazine.org/36/on-virtuality-deleuze-bergson-simondon/

Campan, Véronique. "Le geste de se reprendre ou la répétition comme méthode dans le cinéma d'Abbas Kiarostami". *Filmer l'artiste au travail.* Edited by Gilles Mouëllic and Laurent Le Forestier. Presses universitaires de Rennes. 2013. p. 209-222. doi.org/10.4000/books.pur.74928.

Croce, Benedetto. "Benedetto Croce on aesthetics". *Encyclopedia Britannica.* 2014. britannica.com/topic/Benedetto-Croce-on-aesthetics-1990551.

De Assis. Paolo. *Gilbert Simondon's 'Transduction' as Radical Immanence in Performance. Performance Philosophy.* 2017. performancephilosophy.org/journal/article/view/140

Eickhoff, Hajo. *La posture assise et les chaises ou La perte de spiritualité.* Translated by Stefan Kaempfer. 2001. kaempfer.free.fr/Pages/texteshtm/assise.html

Estanguet, Tony. Official speech delivered at the Opening Ceremony of the Paris 2024 Olympic Games. presse.paris2024.org/actualites/discours-officiel-de-tony-estanguet-prononce-lors-de-la-ceremonie-douverture-des-jeux-olympiques-de-paris-2024-90382-e0190.html

Foucault, Michel. *Of Other Spaces*. Published in *Architecture /Mouvement/ Continuité*. 1984 foucault.info/documents/heterotopia/foucault.heteroTopia.en/
Foucault, Michel. *Technologies of the self*. Lecture at University of Vermont in October 1982. foucault.info/documents/foucault.technologiesOfSelf.en/

Fuller, Andy. Juliastuti, Nuraini. *Reading Sideways Press - Sports Culture*. readingsidewayspress.com/category/sports-culture/

Gardner, Nicholas. Saša, Štucin. Cited in: *Pin–Up Magazine*: Issue 23 (Comfort). 2021. p.218.

Rees, Tim and: Abernethy, Bruce. Côté, Jean. Güllich, Arne. Hardy, Lew. Laing, Stewart. Montgomery, Hugh. Warr, Chelsea. Woodman, Tim. "The Great British Medalists Project: A Review of Current Knowledge on the Development of the World's Best Sporting Talent." _Sports Med_ 46, 1041–1058 (2016). https://doi.org/10.1007/s40279-016-0476-2

Rekow-Fond, Lydie. "Rendre le monde à sa mesure- Corps et perception de l'espace." *Érudit - Sens Public - Corps contemporain et espace vécu*. 2017 erudit.org/fr/revues/sp/2017-sp03802/1048852ar/

"The spinozist 'scream': what can a body do?" *The Funambulist*. Edited by Léopold Lambert. 2013. thefunambulist.net/editorials/spinoza-episode-5-the-spinozist-scream-what-can-a-body-do#top

ART_WORKS

Abramoviç, Marina. Online works. ubu.com/film/abramovic-ulay_relation-work.html

Basselier, Laeticia. "Une introduction à l'oeuvre de Lucinda Childs." *Danses aver la plume.* 2016. dansesaveclaplume.com/359093/en-coulisse/359093-une-introduction-a-loeuvre-de-lucinda-childs/

Brautigan, Richard. *All Watched Over by Machines of Loving Grace.* Poem. lilliputreview.blogspot.com/2011/06/bbc-and-richard-brautigans-all-watched.html1967.

Brouwn Stanley. This Way Brown. 1960-1964. Amsterdam. postpoetical.com/this-way-brouwn/

Farocki, Harun. *Paralel II* and *III.* 2014. https://www.harunfarocki.de/installations/2010s/2014/parallel-iii.html

Frangi, Simone. "The athlete is the artist, the artist is the athlete - A reading of Matthew Barney's Hypertrophy." 2012. rheinsprung11.unibas.ch/fileadmin/documents/Edition_PDF/Ausgabe03/vor-einem-bild.pdf

Hordelin, Friedrich. *In lieblicher Bläue.* In *Hymns and Fragments.* Translated by Richard Sieburth. Princeton University Press. 1984.

Jan Ader, Bas. "Compliation of works." www.youtube.com/watch?v=yvnr0cq0ALQ

Langner, Erin. "The Ganzfeld Effect". *The Offing.* 2021. theoffingmag.com/art/the-ganzfeld-effect/

Marcolini, Patrick. *Le mouvement situationniste - Une histoire intellectuelle.* L'Echappée. 2012.

Muybridge, Eadweard. *The Human and Animal Locomotion Photographs.* Taschen. 2010.

Pane, Gina. *Situation idéale : l'artiste entre ciel et terre.* 1969. navigart.fr/fnac/artwork/gina-pane-situation-ideale-l-artiste-entre-ciel-et-terre-140000000067659

Shen Goodman, Matthew. "We Have Decided Not To Die." *Artnews.* 2018. artnews.com/art-in-america/features/decided-not-die-63507/

Random International. *Living Room.* 2022. random-international.com/living-room-variation-i

Rham, Philippe. *Hormonium.* 8th Biennale of Architecture, Swiss Pavilion. Venice. 2002. philipperahm.com/data/projects/hormonorium/

Teshigawara, Saburo. *Here to here.* Original version (1995 premiered in Frankfurt. New version (2007) premiered in Ferrara. epidemic.net/en/art/teshigawara/proj/here_to_here.html

VIDEO/FILM

Bishop, Claire. "Introduction Claire Bishop Is Everyone a Performer?". Amsterdam. 2015. youtube.com/clip/Ugkxv5JwkDI917rZD8uLCjf43c_frVFWHsFo

Bourriaud, Nicolas. Zhong Mengual, Estelle. "S'inspirer, respirer - Ce que le vivant fait à l'art." 2021. youtube.com/watch?v=ywnKfUwBo7I

Megaforce agency for Burberry. *Open spaces*. 2022. youtube.com/watch?v=pIgDRxkuwwg

Mbembe, Achille. "The Holberg Lecture by Achille Mbembe: *The Earthly Community*." youtube.com/watch?v=omx5NuYBxIk&list=LL&index=1

Nat Geo France. "Faster: The Story of Breaking 2." 2017. https://www.youtube.com/results?search_query=the+stroy+of+breaking+two

Oshii, Mamoru. "Ghost in the Shell Boat Scene." From 1995 film. youtube.com/watch?v=ryJSu1f8Hi4

Seiler, Stephen. "How 'normal people' can train like the worlds best endurance athletes". 2019. youtube.com/watch?v=MALsI0mJ09I

RadioFrance - *Les chemins de la philosophie - Philosophie des arts martiaux - Épisode 2/4 : Judo, karaté, aïkido : comment suivre la Voie ?* 2021. radiofrance.fr/franceculture/podcasts/les-chemins-de-la-philosophie/judo-karate-aikido-comment-suivre-la-voie-9475163

Rosa, Hartmut. "Resonnance and alienation. Two modes of experiencing time?" 2019. https://www.youtube.com/watch?v=57hqmqyQfdk

Tarkovsky, Andrei. *Stalker*. 1979.
Tarkovsky, Andrei. *Solaris*. 1972.

EXHIBITIONS/EVENTS

Italy: The New Domestic Landscape. MoMA. New York. 1972.

Izozaki, Arata. *Ma - Espace/Temps au Japon.* Musée des Arts Décoratifs. 1978.

On Track Nights. on.com/en-gb/explore/events/on-track-nights?srsltid=AfmBOor4SlRW4_ysmcQ94tGBfUSN8tXBzuUMSGJ0HtOFsdjQD1ap6jVX

Superstudio. La vie après l'architecture. Frac Centre. Orléans. 2019.

Mode et sport - D'un podium à l'autre. Musée des Arts Décoratifs. 2024.

www.ingramcontent.com/pod-product-compliance
Lightning Source LLC
Chambersburg PA
CBHW022027290426
44109CB00014B/777